SLOW FIRE

PAMELA ALEXANDER

AUSABLE PRESS
2007

Design and composition by Ausable Press
The type is Sabon with Papyrus titling.
Cover design by Rebecca Soderholm
Author photo by Ed Seling

Cover art: Jennifer Sullivan Carney
"Pond 9: Lily Pad." Acrylic and pastel on paper.
8¼" x 5½." Ucross, Wyoming 1994

Published by
Ausable Press
1026 Hurricane Road
Keene, NY 12942
www.ausablepress.org

Distributed to the trade by
Consortium Book Sales & Distribution
1045 Westgate Drive
Saint Paul, MN 55114-1065
(651) 221-9035
(651) 221-0124 (fax)
(800) 283-3572 (orders)

The acknowledgments appear on page 95 and constititute
a continuation of the copyright page.

Library of Congress Cataloging-in-Publication Data

Alexander, Pamela
Slow fire / Pamela Alexander. –1st ed.
p. cm.
ISBN 978-1-931337-34-2 (trade paper: alk. paper)

I. Title.

PS3551.L3574S56 2007
811'.54–dc22
2006039834

SLOW FIRE

♣

Aries   *1*
New Hampshire Duet   *2*
Letter Home   *4*
Hard Light   *5*
Song   *7*
♣

From the Bastide   *11*
♣

Couple at the Club   *19*
Trash   *21*
Blues   *23*
Crossing   *24*
♣

Local News   *29*
What the Trail Says   *30*
N   *33*
Practice   *35*
Woods that Won't   *37*
Sonoran   *39*
♣

South of Mae West   *45*
Fore   *46*
Cross Wind   *48*

Nest   50

What's Up   51

The Half of It   52

Moonset   53

A Way   54

Here We Are   56

♣

Semiotics   61

Them Bones   62

Person of   65

Things   66

Agenda   69

Logjam Insomnia   71

Big Screen   73

Over the Edge   74

St. Cloud and the Drifters   75

Lightfall   76

Begettery   79

Round   82

♣

Dingle Way   85

Acknowledgments   95

ARIES

I woke in spring. My mother hummed a song
I can't recall. The birds got up. The sun
made shadows, long at first, then sharpened them

to points beneath each tree. She wrote down days
and they made years. Her song got words; the words
got books. I carried them to school and back,

and they got big, and so did I. She sent
me cards from Ocracoke, Tahiti, Maine.
I woke one spring to find my mother dying

gently. One by one she put her words
down, too hard to lift. And then she loosed
the years, which flew away, light as light.

Can make hay into a heifer
but not the other way. Piano
stands on tiptoe to reach a higher note.
Afraid of lightning, wears
glass slippers. She's just a *baby* grand.

I don't turn the light on yet. Outside
conifers wave as if they know me, woods
of my mother's childhood. Who watched hawks
turn. Hurricanes. The moon broadcasting
stammers of ice. A century just begun,
she had to make everything herself, even
heat. Built from sticks,
from air. Made us up, one by
four. Put books to hand
and an upright. Felted hammers! Woodshine!
The tuner couldn't come, notes fell over and broke.

She liked fields of silence with offsprings
of music. Hung suet for the birds, waxy fat
in mesh bags, fuel for whistles
beyond glass. We ate with forks,
knife against the bone.
                    No
finding her anywhere now. Not
in wood, nor air.

Lamplight turns
the night inside out, makes a day in the middle
of dark woods, white keys. Brass, engraved:
Anthony Warfield built this instrument
1929. In 1929 she is
25. Her hands press the keys. The night
steps away to listen. The keys
don't move. She is gone. She presses.

I can't write you because everything's
wrong. Before dawn, crows swim
from the cedars: black coffee calls them down,
its bitter taste in my throat as they circle,
raucous, huge. Questions with no
place to land, they cruise yellow air
above crickets snapping
like struck matches. My house on fire, crows

are the smoke. You've never left me.
When you crossed the river you did not
call my name. I stood in tall grass
a long time, listening to birds
hidden in reeds, their intricate songs.

The grass will burn, the wrens,
the river and the rain that falls on it.
I can go nowhere else: everything
I cannot bear is here.

I must listen deeper. Sharpen my knife.
Something has changed the angles
of trees, their color. Do not wait to hear
from me. I cannot write to you
because this is what I will say.

HARD LIGHT

In a blizzard of heat I admire
insensible buildings: sunlight is hard
and they are harder. I cannot believe
we will see each other again.

Swallows score the air. Inside, in
louvered light, it is eleven—the clock
sings electronically. On its face,
in place of numbers, pictures.
Hour of dove, hour of mockingbird.

Old buildings will be torn down
and the new buildings will look like
each other. Two or three species
of bird will perch in four kinds of tree.

Already I do not care where I am.
I see where you have gone, leaving no
way to follow. Nor can I go back
to the rafts of trillium afloat
in spring woods, to the field where
woodcock courted, high, in spiralled falls,
to your hand turning a frond
to find the rows of spores.

We found a nest with eggs once
in the pocket of a scarecrow. Shall I
look for you there?

I would empty the pockets of the wind.

The clock is broken. It points to
one bird and a different bird sings.

For us it is no time.

SONG

Silence between moons. Notes
for the phoebe round in her nest.
Pitch of roof, pouch of twigs. Words

for nobody. Trees stir like this
for any creature, me or the doe I can't see.
She sees me. Trees wave in the dark.

Postcard with the message crossed out,
all picture. See the song? Earth plays
bass. The moon turns a corner.

FROM THE BASTIDE

the walled town of Puycelsi, Midi-Pyrénées

Stone village brightened by wooden shutters
painted blue. The glass opens inward,
lace panels swaying.

Yesterday, at dawn, a small bat flew inside to rest.

I often talk to the past as if to a child, hoping
it will learn. Now I must talk to the present also
because it happens in two languages.

I am a stranger. Where is the post office? The store?
What color is the sky in this country?

Narrow streets. Lean past lace, past blue, take
a peach from the facing neighbor's table.

The bat

As I think again of the bat, write *The bat,*
the bat flies in. Audible landing.
It crawls behind the bureau, clings.

Songs in the square at night. Beyond the walls,
stars. Owls. Lyrics mostly in English.

Dear C, You are not interested in being with someone. You are interested in the appearance of being with someone.

There is no bread here on Mondays.

//

The men at the bar have sheep shit and straw
stuck to their boots. They are drinking beer
against the sound of rain at ten in the morning.

The dog lies on the stone floor, ears up,
alert idiom. He calls himself Idiot.

The store is not open much. The post office
less. (Dear C, You are pond scum—)
Village so small it's all edge, far above fields
white with mist at dawn.

By noon some of the mist has stayed
as sheep. Other fields dissolve to
sunflowers: crop and ornament.

Foreigner, she leaves the fruit and eats the plate.

Now there is an argument in the bar, everyone
vehement. Good to be "English," ignored.
Don't want to go outside; the rain would notice me.

Foreigner, she ate a horse.

Dear C, You are an artist all right.

Reading in bed: the book opens the window. When she
falls asleep, the window closes.

The words line up, ready;
no moment surprises. I load phrases,
a future pretending to be the present.

Otherwise.

Have you seen the button from my wolf? I have lost him.

Yesterday a white day, no shadows. We wandered,
counting waterfalls and losing count. Butterflies
in zones as we climbed. Black at first; in the high meadows,
yellow, or pale blue with white edges. Fewer
at the rocky summit, and all white.

Back late. A stone on the doorstep
turns into a toad. Sparkling
wine and cous-cous

and the town loud with tinsel music
from a little fair. Its carousel
crowded with spaceships, motorcycles,
tanks with guns. Just one paltry dragon
and something like a llama.

Sixty-year-olds dance
under strings of colored lights.
The music follows us home, upstairs, to bed.

//

The bar's window looks to a slant of hill. Some clouds
drift left to right, like reading, so I see them first.
Some clouds go the other way.

The clock strikes twice each hour. It just struck twelve.
In a few minutes it will be noon again.

Oh, Mother, You should have seen the butterflies!
Different colors for different altitudes, like signage
—a good thing, since the trails weren't otherwise
marked. My pack was green, his orange—perhaps
the butterflies read us too. —Dear C, Months ago you
        asked if
you were my first foreign lover. Did you think I
told the truth? You certainly didn't. You're an artist
        all right—

Dear Anne, It's raining cats and dogs, and one of the
        dogs
has come in and is lying on the stone floor
like a smart dog, even though his name
is Idiot. Red wine, wet dog smell—

—a con artist. May you
get what you want, the appearance
of love. May you—

Postcard to myself. Dear X, Remember
that the blue paint on the shutters is sticky
and takes your fingerprints,
that owls make the dogs bark,
that so much light and coffee make you dizzy.

Remember to be polite.
Remember not to eat the table, exactly.

You will find your way, you know, or
you will make it.

May we all get more than we
can think to want.

Yes. I would like to rain.

COUPLE AT THE CLUB

The bass goes it alone. The bass goes
by subway. The trumpet shines and swerves,
yellow taxi breaking from the light.

The piano bides its time. The trombone
takes a walk in the rain. Bass
boots it, freight train heading west.

The man hides in his courage. Oh dear me no.
In his fright. Sometimes he wears a hat because
he is British. Sometimes because he is bald.

One tune is tough. Broken glass,
broken teeth in it. The piano does
reconnaissance. The sax loiters, bold.

Sax swelters. Flares. His gin is
on the rocks, his hand scarred.
The drums fall down

the stairs. He puts his anger under his hat.
Under the table. Piano remembers, piano
pounds on the door. Somebody opens

a window. Somebody opens the roof.
Some geese are trumpets
calling down the sky. The snare

stings. Bites. The drums obsess.
He is pretty, he is hard as glass. Piano
remembers everything. So does she.

TRASH

I crumple it up & toss it, the whole
island-empire city with gilt
edges on doormen's caps and
on famous buildings. Grab
its gritty facades, pre- and post-
war, and yank it from its bed
of pipes and rats. Silly-looking rooftop
water tanks leak, aerials flail,
and the poised, expensive stonescapes
lose their balance. Into the trash

taking just one inhabitant, the man who
made up names for me I won't say now
because they made me laugh. Then he
lied. His voice lied, his hands. Hell,
even his cat lied. What kind of guy
is that, who doesn't mention he's been lying
down with someone else for years?
Who lets a friend let slip he's gotten
married? His hats fit badly, and sure enough
the lid's too big. I drag the trash can
to the curb like a funeral, frisbee the lid
after it. Let him swelter in there with the glitz
and good jazz and bad air.

                    On the steps I find
a ball of paper, smooth it flat. Letters stand up

into buildings, none of them very tall.
Lights come on in the windows, smoke
from chimneys, smell of coffee. A bird
in the juniper tree opens its eyes and sings.
Its song says who it is, up front, "like a man."

BLUES

They marry, her friends.
They marry friends. She

has many families,
none her own. Kitchen

matches, Blue Bird
in a box. Her sister

dislikes jazz,
blues: just one thing

after another. That's
life, her mother says. Dear

God, gone. The past burns.
Flare, then sulphur sting.

Ohio Blue Tip. A state
of trains: couplings,

sparks from underbodies.
Strike Anytime.

Birthday candles that won't
blow out. Exploding cigar.

Where are they, honey,
I've looked in all the drawers—

CROSSING

Snow falls. A raven flies through it
and grates out the one curse he knows.
He sets his course above the boulder field
I'll cross soon, its thin track
highlighted with powder, the rest blown clear—
a granite slide, gray-green, steep.
Exposure, it's called, when what's above
is rock and what's below, air.

A tall, sharp place. I need it. One path,
clean of guilt and second-guessing—

I'm on it. The wind hasn't left
much snow but my skis float
along the narrow ledge that cuts
straight as a piece of tape. The hard part
is forgetting all else is cocked—
vast tilt of rock above right ear, deep nothing
at left ankle. The hard part's forgetting.

In the middle of something I glide
to a stop. I'm an edge, a balance of going
and going against. I hold the storm down
by one corner, ground it with my weight.
I wear it.

        In the woods the snow wanted
to complicate me: everywhere I looked
looked like trail. Now I know

where I have to go and the knowing stings
like anger. I am a stone
at the bottom of a blizzard, eye
of a raven flying though it. I am rock
and sky and the seam that marries them.

LOCAL NEWS

Grass points. Sycamores elaborate, but why
should I listen? Despite their advice I age faster.
Under their long appointments with themselves
I run errands.
              Dirt composes
rumors I will lie down with it for a song.
I shut a big door against such bawdiness
then open it to drag the philodendrons outside,
their pots full of fibrous wreaths. Let the sky
water them. The driveway glistens
like crushed insects, ants tap their feelers
as if counting the fallen. They're easily distracted,
having only one mind to share among thousands
of feet. I heft my two boots over the threshold
and sit down like a city and have no peace: I hear
the moon get up, a mockingbird practice
all night, trees expand into air and earth.

WHAT THE TRAIL SAYS

First, prepositions. Up, alongside,
under. Then nouns: rock,
tree. Lizard.

Sentences take time.

//

Come here.

Be quiet.

//

Be more quiet and I will
show you something.

Nothing you can hold.

//

Trust rock before dirt, dirt
before scree. Leaf litter
not at all.

//

I am the earth that waits.
You are the earth that walks.

//

Forest of white trees.
A generosity of stars.
Sometimes a snake.

//

Walk until you walk
out of thinking, until
you become walking.

I will be your body, birds and animals
your thoughts.

//

Desert pavement. Above
treeline, rock garden.

I talk to you when you are alone.

//

//

You do not own the breath that moves you
nor its movement.
You have been given to it.

You do not own the slow
fire of your cells, the respiration
of trees.

//

I am made of earth

but not only earth. Like you.

//

You have me
for the moment.

N

One needle steadies
a wilderness of needles.

//

The white pine shimmers all over
like fur.

Facile,
          silvery, the stream wavers,
gravity's errand-girl.

                    Birches
do better. Each declares
an angle, is swayed
only slightly.

But they are many
and do not agree.

Quartz seam
marbling granite, greasy
in the lean scarp—

where it points none walks.

//

Underfoot & gone
a trail crosses the mind
like a forgotten name glimpsed.

Bar of sunlight plants itself
among the pines, transcendental
pine.

//

At noon, stand
on shadow-shoulders and walk

headwards. An hour later
let the shadow fall to the right
15 degrees—

        the straightest line
of reasoning is not human.

//

Slip trump from pocket, needle
housed and mounted on a bearing, free:

Zero degrees
        cuts clean.

PRACTICE

1

A large blue room, one leaf
on the bare floor.

Large blue leaf.

2

The leaf rises, finds
the place a tree once gave it.
Pins itself to air.

3

The stone is granite, composed of several stones.

Its mica glitters, flakes of sun on water.
Quartz glows, blade of a knife
overboard. Feldspar likes

the long nap of geologic afternoons.

4

The stone is composed.
It is the most private form of fire

and the size of a heart.

5

The cricket has practiced all morning.
It can't be any more of a cricket.

It wants to be tall grass, too,
and a warm day, no birds.

6

The stone lifts itself
to the top of the mountain.
The spot it covered is still damp.
The sun beetles above it, large blue light.

WOODS THAT WON'T

My house is depressed. It ate
too much, cupboards stuffed.
To set a good example I take
a walk, find tracks, imagine
the skinny legs of deer.

I wear loud boots and clothing
made of words. My wisdom's
small; I tuck it in a pocket. It grows
heavier with every step.

The crow flies in the middle
of itself. The crow is moving and still,
like a river that flows and holds
the colors of sky and reeds.

No deer shows itself, nor
the bush on fire that is the fox,
nor the dull-eyed porcupine.
Peering at tracks, I see
even my present is past.

Only a dropped hat crouches
in the path. The hat says
Go home, furless one.

In the cold woods I say Quick! Be!
and am unchanged. I say See
and Now. They are the same word.
I remain mind on a stem, talk-talky.

The woods are closed. Will I go back
to the house, servant of my comfort,
and serve it? Acquire, arrange,
decorate? Oh my house will
be pleased. It will have me
in for dinner, will lower its shades
and prop a sprig of smoke
over its chimney pot.

I gather my wits in a heap
on the ground. They are
few. Under them I light a match.

SONORAN

Sky tilts, the south enlarges.

Rivers run with sand,
sand and heat-shimmer.

Days away, staggered,
the mountains.

//

Blood's both water and fire,
liquid that feeds the body's
slow burn, cell-fire.

Something like a sound.
Something like a sound so faint
it's noticed only when it stops.

//

In Maine I lost my way
on rock, in snow,

in fog. Here I've lost
the self that finds the way.

//

No place is home for long.

//

Walk under fire, over
fire. Hard ground.

Creosote, sage,
plants like standing flames.

//

Time hums. Has a small song.

//

Over the rise, a rancher's bone-dump:
sketches for horse, for sheep.

//

Time carries, and carries, and tires
of us. One by one. Sings us down.

//

You can't say *I don't like this life*
and walk away from it into your past.

No place is home.

//

Let it stand nevertheless: wrote *fog*,
read *joy*.

SOUTH OF MAE WEST

Oh boy aubade, a wide one, me in Ohio
you in Tucson. Met you in the desert with a radio
in your pack, cacti let you by and then bit me;
my socks still bristle botanically. I'm snagged
by your orange anorak and scree gaiters, obsessed
by your fanny pack and your fanny, dammit.
You were over my head, your heels rising
on thermals, must've been, no footholds I could see.
Saw ammo on the dash but when I asked if you were
packing you said A highly improper question.
I'm feeling highly improper. Antenna standing up and
quivering, is that *de rigueur?* Boy oh baby, it's
the morning of something. Haven't been inside your
truck or trailer, you haven't been inside my—was that a
hoodoo in your pocket or were you just glad to see me?
You speak good German which means you like to save
all your verbs for dessert. Not me, I like 'em everywhere
and active. I like your syntax, Sylvester all over.
You ran up rocks like a cat burglar, well
burgle me. My alarm's disarmed.

FORE

i

(1)self: upstanding
ego, aye. Stroke
of genius, luck, what-
have-you, strikes out on its
only go. Mast-like in the midst
of flurry, sails and all, windfall.
Or nothing much: the ordinary
life. Is there such a? Hands
full, headful of imaginary,
like numbers. Go on, square
one: still upstart I.

ii

A couple of things you ought
to know about 2: it's tight,
the knot let no one
etc. Hats off,
shirts. Urgency abroad
in the body—cathedral arch
of groin, striped-maple-striped
muscles, blood chemistry lighting up
lighthouse brain. Two's a trip, you're It
for the long haul: equal parts

giggling fits and the face
of, after all, mortality (against
which you know what counts & who).

iii

Three cheers for hoo
met & married. He
said she said hip
hip. Not knowing how

they done it, they done:
I do then daily
does, all kind. Dear
dear. The tallest dawn

wakes them deep. Ups
manship, Oh woman oh
my. Redbirds whoop,
foxes yip, she Oops

it slipped, then fit all ways.
Together is one. They is.

CROSS WIND

My dear curmudgeon, grousling,
growlycat, where the hell
are we? Out the window,

flatland—rich as a pan of fudge
scored into squares—shoots
its sugar into corn and beans

and so few trees it's hard
to call them *woods*. Perhaps
a wood? The wood that hedges

the fields is scarcely as deep as
a deer is long, so how a buck hides
its hide from hunters

we can't think. (We infer from
trucks full of fluorescent men
there's more than one buck.)

Roads run in cardinal directions,
Cartesian grid. We move along x
and y; z is for crows. *What's up?*

is not a tactful question here.
Town's so small you know everyone,
even people you don't. Rain

pocks mud. When the cellar
pump shakes our sleep we call out
Man the lifeboats, she's going down.

Down she's going. Wanted
to know what it meant to throw
caution to the wind. It means

living in a windy place.
Thought she understood
the word *smitten,* but no.

The plains get plainer. Something's
loose. The hypotenuse squared
is the whole rest of the state. Dear

y, is this our home, ark, our
covenant? Pussycat, grumpster, sweet
hypothesis, I find myself blowing away.

NEST

Their little furs meet, make much
of each, you know the story, old
as hills, being silly up and down
the length of them. They get along

and then relapse. Autumn. Hard-headed
cyclists fly by in gangs; wasps
drift through the high white rooms
to bang against glass. Never learn.

Clouds smuggle the sun across, tea's
cold. They've lost their places in the books
on the bed, the bed's rucked up. Some
thing's humming that isn't them.

And rain. Worse, it's raining
wasps. Not the wings they want.

WHAT'S UP

See you on the other side, he says, rolling
over, turning out his light. I read a while

then put the book aside, spine up, roof
over a house of words, over spirits of trees.

Out all night. Where am I going? And those
people—do I know them? Must, they're me.

We can walk up the road and down;
we can wake only up. Mostly we don't notice

becoming ourselves again, the ordinary
given into our hands, a warm loaf, full cup,

light getting up and changing everything.
Morning, he says, as if nothing's happened.

THE HALF OF IT

Rain falls into my hair. It falls
into my coffee, which I drink,
thinking rain, becoming
rain. I sit on the rocks
(as we say of drinks and
ships, including relationships),
watching waves wave
and not waving back.
Some people can't live without
an ocean, some require mountains.
Some have to have each other

and some want something smaller:
a rock to talk to, a place to sit
where nothing happens. Nothing's
hard to find. Wherever a tree falls
philosophies sprout. The sky
can fall, and when it does
two get twice as wet as one.
No half's the better.

Now there's more rain in my coffee
than coffee. Birds are singing but what
do they know? In spring they
get fat, fall into nests and
yadder out songs. Lovely. Doomy.
Usness doesn't last like I'd like
to think. Birds say it's seasonal,
rain knows it's all downhill.

52

MOONSET

Something stirs: perhaps a farm dog
gruff behind the darkness of tall corn,
or roosters ruffled in their sleep
by dreams of dawn. Impossible
to see the steep black road; his feet
feel it out. No sound
but gravel, sometimes, shifting
under his boot. Too late, too late

to sleep. Fog dims a streetlight
like a lampshade; in the milky cone
his shadow stands beside him.
He set out under clouds luminous
with a full moon; now, red, it melts
at the horizon.

          The hills catch
whispers of light from west,
from east. A day he should welcome--
lovely, the red moon going under, fields
just visible, undulating in mist—
and he will, though he sees it's too late
to have a life he cares about.

A WAY

She takes the road out
of her suitcase and unrolls it.
Not a very good road. Turns
it over; the other side is just
as bad. She works as she walks
along it, pulling things from pockets
to fill the holes—boats, houses,
big words, rhododendrons, awkward
philosophies.

              She's forgotten
where she told it to go; besides,
who's to say it's well-behaved?
It hasn't said a thing. Prone
to depression, of course. Probably
imagines her wishing she'd picked
some other road. Which
she does. At her feet

a crevasse opens, deeper than
she can think. She has nothing left
that's big enough. The kind of compass
you draw circles with. Matchbox
of angers. Keys. Loose wishes.
What kind of road are you? she asks.
No answer.

The sky turns the color
of a wet rat's fur. Thought she'd get
somewhere and all she's gotten is
tired. She lies down and watches
the moon rise. The road stirs. *My
hero*, it sighs—*look at her! All I want
to be—high and round and bright.*

HERE WE ARE

Today it is. Right here next to
yesterday which, wanting

to be perfect, fell down. Today's
morning opens big doors

but doesn't know what to do
with itself. It has a chair and a hill

and a window between. It can look out
and in. Nothing sits in the chair, nothing

moves on the hill. Beyond the hill
is a darker hill, but today hasn't

gotten that far.
                    I am around here
somewhere. Today tries the chair,

stands at the window. It stands
on the hill, too, talking to itself

with the sound of daylight.
It stops wondering what

to do: it has half a planet to get to
and the half keeps moving. It has

to make hay, it has to make trees.
I am a here. A standing. I hold

sky in my hands, which are empty,
which have let slide the economy

of clocks. Now is an economy
of air. It has abundance but is not

full. It stands around me. I stand
around it. Now it is.

SEMIOTICS

Rain falls between the notes
the violist in the next apartment plays.
He's one quarter of a distinguished quartet
that hasn't much English; you pass
the same word back and forth. Hello!
What is there to say? The world is dumb
and sings. The world is dumb and speaks
in its big dumb voice that sometimes sounds
like a viola, very nice. Sometimes like diesels. Or
it insists on sign language, waving seasons around
like busy flags. What does it mean that
your heart gets hiccups? The world wants you
to speak its language and you don't know
American Sign or Universal Sign, certainly not
Cosmic Sign. Now your heart wants
an interview. It scribbles madly
on the monitor, giving itself a polygraph test
and failing grandly, proud that it lies.
It never thinks ahead. You're its wrapper,
its bathrobe, and it loves you deeply
but can't remember your name.

THEM BONES

In prehistory, pre-
hensile. Now stubs
stuck into old boxes.

Arches, keyless.

First, patter: the whole thing down flat.
Then each step two-stepped, flexed.

Game stalkers.

Underdogs.

Do ankles have ears? As owls
have ear-tufts.

Shinny
straight up: tall drink of water.

Hinges. How useful to be half
as tall

or horizontal, functions
redefined: behind the knees
where the cat sleeps.

Slightly curved, curve

obscured, fat cells piled alongside
like dirty dishes.

Ship's bow half-submerged, pelvic
flare. Watery, and salt,
and surge.

Somebody didn't stack them straight,
these osteo-
knots. But they balance

and the long wires drop through them.

Home is where you hang
your heart. It bangs against the rails,
all id, kid in a crib.

Boilerplate sternum and beamy
collarbones.

The scapular even the laity wears

supports distal swimmers in air, radials

to the fiddlers and rustlers, famous
gang of two. Getters. Fixers.
Overreachers.

Hey! You'd need a couple of
hundred thousand each
barrels of biochemicals, a warehouse
of industrial spools of neural and
vascular tissue, nine months
under a heart lamp.

Bonehead, you've got
the life you always wanted. Make it
a good one. Make it worth dying for.

PERSON OF

Person of water, eye-shine, thigh-
sweat, person of
air in a skinny bag, breath
in bone-box, person moving in plumes
of bodyheat, person

of candor, ambition, dread,
webbed with minerals, cartilage, who
remembers the house, its lights, how
it stood to the road,
how the road was black and shone
when rain described the air,
how the kitchen clanged an hour
before dinner, aluminum anger, who
ate from the pot and remembers

how what was said was said, how
it cannot be unheard, person

of doings and undoings,
woman of water and sand, of chairs
and coffee, silence and wishy talk,

woman of liquors, odors, airs,
lion of walking, sky of waiting,
woman cloudy, woman dappled,
woman broad as daylight.

THINGS

when the mother died
two of them took her things
filled their houses
didn't want them, wanted not
to discard them

the other two didn't want anything
because they'd had much
spent and bought and so on
discard was part of what they did

the one with the most of the mother's things
had leaves on her stove
newspapers in her sink
her phone wouldn't talk

this is how the meek inherit
they get things they don't want

//

I start collections every day

have to like the surface, the design,
the American ingenuity

could teach history without books

put some thing in their hands
and people just get it

cases of Bush and Rumsfeld dolls
make the Iraq War real

still in the package

it's about authenticity

sure space is a problem
I've got a barn, a couple sheds

can live with these things forever
a passion, I'm an artist at heart

just had to find the ladyfriend who
would buy into my dream

//

at Christmas the family had a potlatch
too many toys to fit into the car

petroleum to plastic to Elmo the guitarist
who plays rock music, flashes red and green

wooded hills were destroyed but
he didn't cost much

artificial planet in a haze
of debris, space junk

we can talk to satellites
and stars—no wonder

we're unamazed

I'm no hero on this count—
counting car, computer, microwave,

"air conditioning" (advertising
language become unremarkable)

I have seen eleven foxes in my life

This day I am ashamed of my kind

AGENDA

Let's build a house.
Let's build a bigger house.
Let's build a hundred very big houses
in rows. No, closer. Okay, let's

sell them to each other, build
another bunch. If we turn
outdoors inside out,
we'll be in. Did you
say something?

Outdoors needs doors.
In Xanadu did Kubla Khan.
A man's home is his palace, I mean
a person's house is his/her palace.

The outdoors is great. Look at it
through this window.
It goes well with the rug doesn't it?
Do you think we need to change
anything?

What did you say?
I thought I heard something.
I thought we had a deal.
You're not sold on this one?

Wait. The voice is louder.
Voices. Do you think they
want to buy? Maybe—
not. They're saying something
that sounds like *earth*,
something that sounds like *war*.

LOGJAM INSOMNIA

The palm is potted, the cat drunk
on nip, little leaves all over the floor.
Leaves make wood makes nuts
that taste like woody food.

Bedtime! Put out the cat,
say goodnight to the light.
The radio is trained to put itself
to sleep. It says the time is green.

It says *the execution rate is up* and Texas
is why. *Texas is dealing with a back
log.* Did the radio say *black?* The cells
are concrete and the bars more so.

First war and then wars, abroad,
at home, we're losing count—
people who aren't, everywhere.
Street fights, drive-by shootings. The car

took a sharp right. The court went right
hard. *The court is not interested in criminal
law.* It accepted ten cases of something else, broke
for lunch. Shrimp fettuccini, Chablis. Did the radio say

lynch? It's a fine court. Their honors know
their shrimp and need their rest. Would they sit
longer if they had only wood to eat? They have
their moods, historically. Eventually we'll be fine

as wine, as a split hair, fine as all the print
fit to be news, that old story. Get the cat in,
put the light out. Tell the radio when to tell us
to up our ante. We put good money on

making somebody pay. The prisoner wants
a Big Mac and, more, the woods beyond MacDonald's.
He got the short end of the gavel. If mountains
won't move, maybe woods? He'll pass muster

and then a lot of bars, acres of wood on the hoof.
He'll slip among the trunks like a brilliant weasel.
The bulldozers won't wake up, he'll laugh out loud
and pass the hat, the buck, the joint. He'll pass time.

BIG SCREEN

The boys who hit the boys
are making movies.
One show only, playing
here and now.

The boys get big, make girls
bigger. Knock
their kids around a bit.
Good for them, they'll see.
Boys will beget boys.

The street is dark until
the stars come out
to find their pals and make
a scene. The boys who shoot
the boys do camera time.

The late show's live,
the lives are cast. Lights.
Sirens. Photo ops. Cops and
watch it. Cut. Cut.

OVER THE EDGE

Quoth the poet, Looky here.
Lo and behold and like that.
O.K., we be we hold we sally
duly forth. Hang around

like crows and critics. Got things
sorta sorted out, water goes
with salt and fishes and oily
ships; scratchy cats and bushes

in a bunch. We got mountain tops
with mountains unnerneath,
neat. Rivers every whichway though.
Got critters, Cryptosporum,

cities, crepes suzette, saxophones
warm and breathy, trees—
about here sumpin happens,
beauty change us bad. In cahoots

with our own selfs, natch,
bodies and what they do
to us. Nevermind
language what changes

out from under. Nothing firm
about terra. We're on a roll.

ST. CLOUD AND THE DRIFTERS

                    So this cloud digresses
right through the window, settles on the blue
yoga mat. Don't get too comfy, I say.
Come spring the city's pulling this house down
—me and the skunk in the cellar
looking for a new place.
                         Chill, says the cloud. Hold
that chair over your head: a forest. Put it down
while thick-necked horses drag trees to the mill
before you were born. Pick it up again, there's
your roof. Think where hawks hang out,
where sheep sleep. Man, you've got it made
in the rooftree's shade.
                         That's a neat trick,
I say. How about you hustle me up some sheetrock
too? If there are wolves, I need walls.

                              The cloud
weeps openly. The earth is an animal, it says,
one animal, continuous. I am your tears.

LIGHTFALL

All the light was north, snow on skylights,
the year I lived in the painter's studio.

Scrub forest behind the dunes, a litter
of deer tracks and shotgun shells.
I tied an orange bandanna around
the husky's neck.

//

I knew the dark place was wrong. I walked the letters
of my name, which I did not recognize spoken.

Low corridors.
Me. Her. The I
I could not find.

All the trees had fallen the same way
in the storm. A landscape pointing.

Anyone could happen like that.

//

The husky ate a bee
out of the air, snapped herself shut
on compound eyes, wing-blur, button
of darkness and buzz.

//

A rabbit streaked from under my feet.
Its nest fit my loose fist.
A cup of winter grass, still warm.

Home is the first everywhere,
the place we go out from.

//

The bee flew lower. Pollen graining its legs
drizzled onto linoleum shine. The room

was a different color for each of us. My shadow
bright blue-green in bee sight.

How could it not recognize the window
colored *open?*

//

I longed to be among trees. They wavered
beyond glass, beyond wire. They could not
be changed into words. They could not be changed
into anything. Even a camera couldn't see
the thick air around them, how it carried
sounds whole like water does,
how it supported slow birds.

//

Bee against pane, translucency
of wings. Centuries flew
against the glass. Then we found
the larger place: earth, that blue ark
afloat in the wilderness of space.

We cannot count ourselves out.

//

How beautiful it was
before we knew. How sweet how

A faint music falls from the stars—

no it does not.

BEGETTERY

Begat begat begat

saw an angel in the sun, said
we cannot live in a community of one
species

started when I was about 10 my mother said Imagine
I am always watching you and I did after a while
adding other people I liked in the corner of the room
on the street commenting approving it's lasted all this
time a habit I choose the people some of them dead
now I call them human angels

go forth and multiply Replenish
the earth

the plow turned up roots of the grasses we had burned
it made a sound like tearing cloth

how the light has changed across
the desert, across
centuries

cultivated
then mined subdivided paved sold

Nature passé
market factor
pet, poor panda, baby seal: the eyes
win us, warm fur Who'd love a lobster? worm?

double-minded man
too fast too slow

you know I am always en passant in my little red truck

Done because there were too many (Dickens)

having killed the other predators, we have ourselves left to

a double minded man is unstable in all his ways (James 1:8)

at a loss impasse
a fall from

good piano in an abandoned loft

god we made it shake the whole place was us man
was music a way to be beyond ourselves a new way
we made as we went oh that place was shakin we
shook it loose the building shoulda fallen down and
if it had we woulda played all the way woulda kept
jammin

what we did was save ourselves
for a moment

the way of writing is crooked and straight
(Heraclitus)

correct rock-climber's call when falling is Falling

found my dear aunt's diary in her house after the
funeral A fine day, mild or Rained all day, cold
wind Just years of weather

well that's what we get
weather, a few moments
falling through time

ROUND

Boats we are. The light
we float on rises, ebbs.

Weather is water

and its ways. It's where
we live, big
blue planet

in our heads. Light
washes in.

Out. The life
we float on. Boats.

DINGLE WAY

for my sister, who stayed home

If not for the politics of famine, we
would have been born here.

Could tell a Dublin car from a Tip.
Poont from pound; now they're both
Euros. Oh, her
literary bent. Rub two

words together for a plot: where, because.

Story story. The long
and the short of it.
The part about the mother
has to come first.

She opened the light for us
like a book. Spine cracked.

First, about the mother.
(You say everything twice.)
I know, I know.

After supper she stood
in the field. Looking at the sky.
At nothing. Stood until

Books in the museum: made of bark,
of jade. Rope, rice.

//

If not for. Early beside the house
an owl called. Eerily an owl. My first Irish.

The story way. The way here.
Who did what of course. Who's related,
can't leave that out. Families
grow on trees. Where's she from?

Prayers can be *to*. They can also be *of*.

My husband's from here,
his mother's kin shipbuilders
and lighthouse keepers. (I knew
the sea'd get in here somewhere.
Inlets.) It's an island. He can't swim.

Rampant on a sea of

Our mother's family, rampant on a field of

Buddhists copied prayers to please
the gods. Handwritten strips fluttered
from branches. Trees make good messengers
in both directions.

Then invented block prints for faster copies.

Two short stories don't make a long one.

(You say everything twice.) Not everything.
(More than twice.) There are reasons.
So does the ocean. (So did she.)

//

People smoke together at the pub, play
chess and Scrabble, later darts, watch
—no, listen to—the telly. It speaks English.

A lovely dinner though we all talk about rats
and bees. Now we walk in the road.
No moon, but the night luminous,
soft, an August sky, as west as you can go
without a boat. The violent high hill
and below us, dimly, islands like freighters, each
trailing its cloud to leeward. Steaming
for port? We're walking in the road
and singing. Tralee, tralee, a place
or a song? Anybody join in.

He said he lay in the field, reading maybe,
and let bees walk on him. Their feet were cold.

Dingle bells, Dingle all the way,
he and I sing later, in the car.

Outside, sheep blur by, shoulders
sprayed a blue that brightens the dun fields.

Field: a piece of land
with an identity. Country, county, field.
How successfully I am neither here nor there.
With him and not. With her.

Hay in black plastic cubes or cylinders.
Abstractions, field of.

//

From the Latin *to speak*, become both
private prayer and public address.

Oratory as prayer hut. Were the prayers
sung? Choir of one. Conical, stones
fitted together in the twelfth century, still
weatherproof. Still

standing, afield. A sign of

//

Air: two angels holding gospel books.

Earth: two mice holding the eucharist,
scrutinized by two cats with mice on their backs.

The Book of Kells looked grimy in the dim light.
Dozens of people crowding, a guard saying
Move along there. Some colors—white lead, red
lead, yellow arsenic—even then
they knew were poisonous.

The cost of memory. Cost of prayer.

Water: an otter with a fish in its mouth.

She stood, said "——." Said
"——." No, I can't
remember what, only
the form of her speaking.

Where is Fire? The page upon which

An old church in ruins, gray in the rain, gray
in the sun. Antenna glistening above it.

Something about its being spoken, you know.
The timing, the timbre, the presence of a voice.
What's written is history.

The Gallatus Oratory. Port
in the invisible storm,
the visible. It has stood aside from
how many wars? Has held its place.

Two figures, the speaker and the spoken,
both disembodied.

As if fire uttered a sound. As if it could
be transcribed.

//

Orthography changed by fiat. Whose.
Not Irish speakers. A form
of assimilation, to make the language fit
for the Internet—familiar to strangers,
strange to its people.

In the country, in Dunquin, in Ballyferriter,
etas and thorns survive. Road signs
handpainted. English underneath, sometimes.

Not everyone does what everyone does.

//

She wrote for herself at first, then for others,
now for herself. A way of living, the living
she makes. Holds herself up to see the light
as it flows. The Liffey in a jar. The Charles.
Mississippi.

I say that in the third person. Who
is that? Someone made up, make believe.
Not here, but here.

//

Western coast again, a room above the rocky edge.
Noon, the hardest light. Sea moiling below, ice
green. Cows low, now and then a dog barks.
Birds, one cat. Sheep. Flies
everywhere, nobody cares.

Wait. Try again. The waves.
The waves hike their white skirts
to jump up on the rocks. The rocks

No, the sea is oily, bread sour.
Holidays are over.

//

Everyone speaks some lines.
Others repeat them. Everyone makes up
a few lines of the book which is
various and vast and anonymous.

ACKNOWLEDGMENTS

Grateful acknowledgement is made to the editors
and publishers of the journals in which many of
these poems first appeared:

Agenda (U.K.): "Aries"
Agni: "What's Up"
The Atlantic: "Couple at the Club"
Boston Book Review: "Blues," "Them Bones,"
    "Semiotics"
Denver Quarterly: "New Hampshire Duet,"
    "Fore," "A Way"
88: "Nest," "Song"
The Journal: "Cross Wind," "The Half of It,"
    "St. Cloud and the Drifters," "Woods
    that Won't," "Over the Edge"
Marlboro Review: "Letter Home," "Practice"
    (as "Studio Poem")
Mid-American Review: "Lightfall"
Orion: "Agenda," "Local News," "N," "Sonoran,"
    "What the Trail Says"
Perihelion: "Dingle Way"
Pleiades: "Here We Are"
Salt River Review: "Hard Light," "South of Mae
    West"
Shenandoah: "Moonset"
Smartish Pace: "Big Screen"
TriQuarterly: "From the Bastide"
Vespertine Press: "Person of"

And thanks to the editors of these anthologies for
reprinting some of the poems:

Best American Poems 2000: "Semiotics"
American Alphabets: "Person of," "Lightfall,"
    "Crossing"

Special thanks to the good people at Centrum,
the Montana Artists Refuge, and the MacDowell
Colony.